The Loose Tooth

By Aziyah Turner

Illustrated by Cameron Wilson

ROYSTON
Publishing

BK Royston Publishing LLC
P. O. Box 4321
Jeffersonville, IN 47131
http://www.bkroystonpublishing.com
bkroystonpublishing@gmail.com

Copyright 2021

All Rights Reserved. No part of this book may be reproduced, stored in a retrieval system, or transmitted by any means without the written permission of the author.

Cover Design and Illustrations: Cameron Wilson

ISBN-13: 978-1-955063-51-7

Printed in the USA

Dedication

This book is dedicated to children everywhere who has and will lose a tooth.

Acknowledgements

First I want to thank God for blessing me with the talents and gifts to do all of these things.

I want to thank my mom, Tamika Nelson for helping me create the story when my 1st tooth was "loose." It was so much fun coming up with characters and having them look the way I wanted them to.

I'd like to thank my Dad, Reggie Turner for believing in me and telling me that I can do & be anything that I put my mind to.

I also want to thank all of my family & friends for all of your love and support.

Introduction

I wrote this book because it was the funniest story that my mom and I made up one night at bed time, when my loose tooth came out. We were laughing so hard at the thought of my tooth being afraid to come out that we wanted to share this story as a gift with everyone.

For more information and to follow on social media,

email us at: Theloosetooth1@gmail.com

Theloosetooth1 on Instagram

Theloosetooth1 on Facebook

Kayla was playing basketball at school with her friends. Mariahly passed Kayla the ball. When Kayla tried to catch the ball, it slipped and hit her squarely in the mouth causing her front tooth to loosen. Kayla was nervous because when she touched her tooth with her tongue, it wiggled a bit.

When Kayla returned home from school, she told her mom and dad all about her day and what happened on the basketball court. Kayla's mom took a closer look at her tooth and discovered that it indeed was loose.

"Oh wow!" her mom exclaimed, "Are you ok, sweetheart?"

"Yes mom, I'm ok, it doesn't hurt that bad," Kayla replied.

Her dad in his deep strong voice said, "Kayla, remember you have to be careful when you're playing with your friends."

"I will," replied Kayla.

After dinner and right before bed,
Kayla goes to brush her teeth as she always does.
"Owww," Kayla winces.

She notices that the bristles from the toothbrush seem to be a little too rough on her gums tonight. She calls for her parents to come and see just how much more her tooth loosened up after she ate dinner.

Kayla's mom took one good look at her loose tooth, then turned to her dad excitedly and said,
"oh honey, I think it's time for someone to hear the story about the Tooth Fairy!"

Dad chuckled, examining Kayla's tooth further and said, "oh yes, I think you're right!"

When it was time for Kayla's parents to tuck her into bed that night, they told her all about how the Tooth Fairy comes to collect all of the teeth when they fall out.

In return for your tooth, she places $5 under your pillow for a gift. Kayla thought that was a pretty cool story, but she was a little nervous about what it would be like to lose a tooth.

After the story, Kayla and her parents recited their prayers and exchanged goodnight hugs and kisses. Kayla's parents turned off her night light and wished her sweet dreams.

Shortly thereafter, Kayla drifted off to sleep.

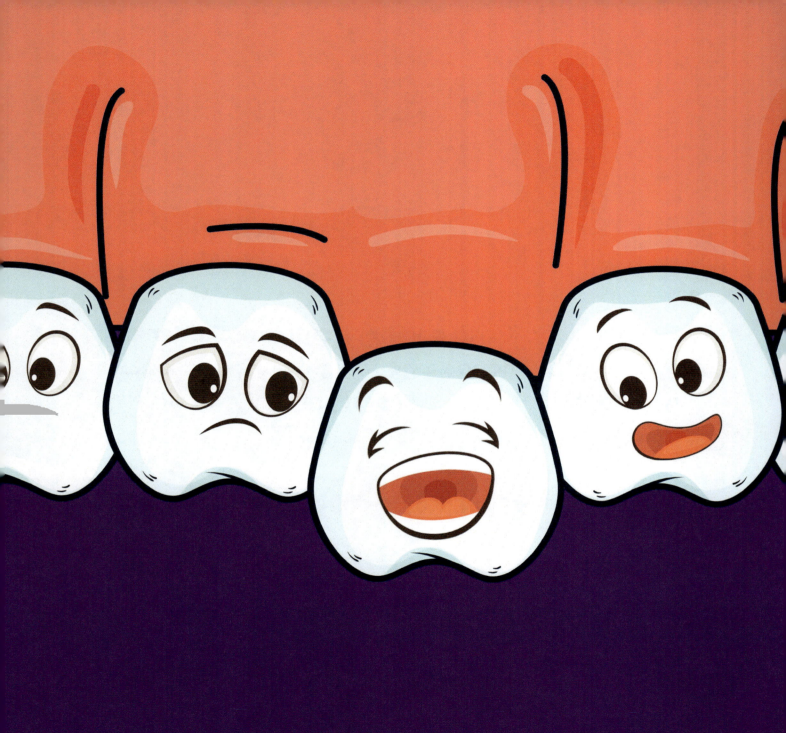

Little did Kayla know, when the Tooth Fairy story is told, the loose teeth become so very nervous!

Suddenly, Pauly, "the loose tooth" of the set looked around at all of his friends and cried aloud, "I don't want to fall out, I want to stay here with you guys!"

Pauly's closest tooth buddy Jack reassured him that everything would be alright, "Hey man, you were the first one to come in so you have to be the first one out. Don't worry I'll join you soon. After all, we won't be as strong when you're not around!" said Jack

At that very moment, all of the teeth pushed tighter to give Pauly one last hug. Unknowingly, causing him to be more loose.

Pauly felt better and began to think about
what it would be like to not have to be so sticky
from all of the candy that Kayla loved to eat.
And how it wouldn't tickle so bad when Kayla would
have to brush him every day and night.
Pauly knew for a fact that he wouldn't miss the minty
cool toothpaste that Kayla used.
Although it kept him sparkly, Pauly hated the taste.

Remarkably, Pauly started to get excited about going to the magical place that he's heard about since he was young.

As Pauly began to get sleepy,
the whole set of teeth sang their goodnight song,
"Twinkle, Twinkle little tooth, how I wonder if I'm loose. When we fall from the gum, the Tooth Fairy will surely come."

Then off they slept.

The very next morning, as soon as the sun peeped through the window, Kayla sat up in bed & touched her tooth to see if it was still there. To her surprise, it was. She smiled, had breakfast and went off to school.

At recess, Kayla decided to play hop-scotch instead of basketball to be more careful like her dad said. As Kayla placed her foot down into the square, she didn't realize that her shoe was untied and tumbled right to ground, face first.
Pauly felt the shaking.

Instead of being afraid he thought 'this is my time to be brave.'

Pauly gave all of his friends one last hug then closed his eyes and jumped right from Kayla's gum and fell out of her mouth.

When Kayla opened her eyes, there was Pauly "the loose tooth" planted right on the hop-scotch square. Immediately, Kayla ran to her teacher to tell her what happened. Mrs. Chelsea cleaned and bandaged Kayla's scrapped knee. She also gave Kayla a tooth container to keep Pauly safe until they made it home.

**Inside the tooth container, Pauly wondered nervously,
'If this dark place was Tooth Fairy land?'**

Once home, Kayla could not keep the excitement to herself. She rushed through the doors with the biggest smile on her face. Pointing to the now empty space between her teeth to show her parents.
Kayla's mom and dad smiled with her and shared a hearty laugh.

"Now, let's put that tooth under your pillow to keep it safe sweetheart," said Kayla's dad!

After dinner, Kayla brushed her teeth as she always does, and boy was it weird. There was no longer a straight line to brush across. There was now a hole. Kayla smiled in the mirror and stuck her tongue through the space.

Kayla's parents tucked her into bed.
They all recited their prayers together and exchanged goodnight hugs and kisses.
Kayla's parents turned off her night light and wished her sweet dreams.
Shortly thereafter, Kayla drifted off to sleep.

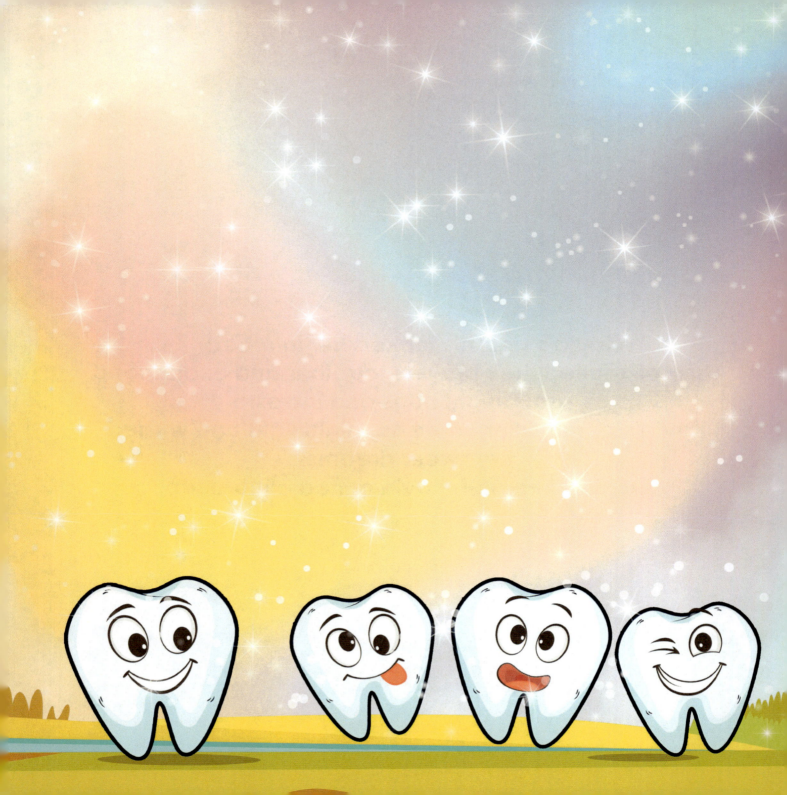

Pauly was nervous and wondered if the Tooth Fairy would ever come? As it has been a very long day for him. Just then the dark room became bright. The pillow was lifted up gently, and Pauly saw the sweet friendly face of the Tooth Fairy.
She picked Pauly up and placed him snuggly in her pouch. In return for Pauly, the Tooth Fairy placed $5 in the space where Pauly was placed. Just like that they were gone.

When Pauly opened his eyes he couldn't believe what he saw. There were pink, yellow and blue fluffy clouds all across the sky. Sparkly teeth where shining bright everywhere.

"Wow, this place is awesome," said Pauly.
A few of his new tooth buddies invited him to play with them, and off Pauly went.

As soon as the sun peeped through the window, Kayla sat up in bed & lifted her pillow to check on her tooth. To her surprise, her tooth was gone but in its place lay a crisp $5 bill.

Kayla raced to the kitchen to show her mom and dad. "Look what I found under my pillow. The Tooth Fairy came last night," Kayla said.

Her parents smiled and hugged her tightly. "What are you going to buy with all of that money?" Kayla's dad asked.

"Ummm, I don't know yet," Kayla pondered.

"Go hurry, and get dressed for school. Afterward, we will take you to the store so you can buy yourself a treat," said Kayla's mom.

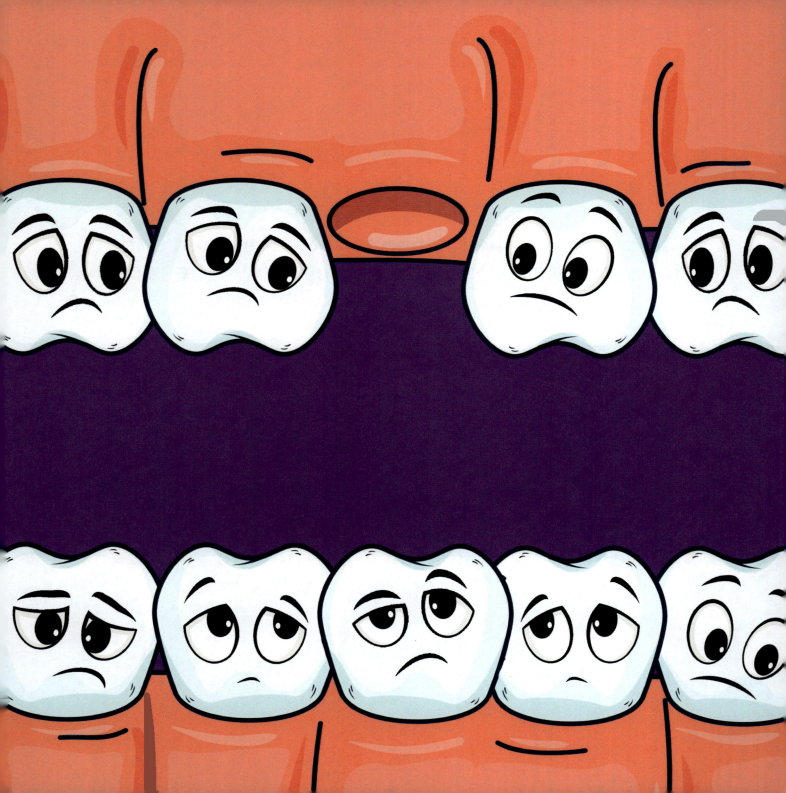

As Kayla brushed her teeth and thought about what gift she might buy herself later at the store.
The other teeth couldn't help but feel sad when they looked over and saw the toothbrush going in and out of the empty space where Pauly once was.
They would miss their friend dearly but they knew he was safe. They also knew that one day they would be joining Pauly in Tooth Fairyland.

Kayla finished brushing her teeth and hurried off to school. She couldn't wait to show off her brand new toothless smile and see all of her friends.

The End.

Made in the USA
Middletown, DE
23 December 2021